A FOURTEENTH-CENTURY PLAY

THE WAKEFIELD RESURRECTION PLAY

Translated from the Middle English and Adapted for Modern Performance by

Cynthia Bourgeault

A CROSSROAD BOOK
THE SEABURY PRESS • NEW YORK

The Seabury Press
815 Second Avenue
New York, N.Y. 10017

Note:

Professionals and amateurs are hereby instructed that this material is protected by copyright law. It is illegal to copy this either in whole or in part.

When this play is produced, a minimum of nine copies must be purchased for the use of the director and actors. Purchase in this quantity serves in lieu of payment of a royalty fee and constitutes permission to produce the play.

ACKNOWLEDGMENTS

Grateful acknowledgment is extended to the following publishers and agents for permission to reproduce copyrighted materials from the sources listed:

W. W. Norton & Company, Inc.—"Rex Coeli, Domine" and "Parce, Domine" from *Masterpieces of Music Before 1750* by Carl Parrish and John F. Ohl. Copyright 1951 by W. W. Norton & Company, Inc. Used by permission.

Library of Congress Catalog Card Number: 73-77769
ISBN: 0-8164-2083-1
Text and cover design by Carl Basen
Printed in the United States of America

Contents

Performers

THE WAKEFIELD RESURRECTION PLAY
is cast for the following performers:

Fourteen speaking actors, as follows:

A CENTURION	FOURTH SOLDIER
PILATE	CHRIST
CAIPHAS	MARY MAGDALENE
ANNAS	MARY SALOME
FIRST SOLDIER	MARY JACOBY
SECOND SOLDIER	FIRST ANGEL
THIRD SOLDIER	SECOND ANGEL

A small angel choir, ideally of about a dozen voices.
A children's choir, also of about a dozen voices.
Three or four pages and flagbearers for Pilate's court.
The following instruments:

snare drum	sopranino (or soprano) recorder
bass drum	organ
gong	

seven handbells in C_4, G_4, C_5, E_5, G_5, A_5, C_6

The children's choir may carry the following additional percussion instruments:

triangle	tambourine
finger cymbals	hand drum

The snare drummer and recorder player are costumed and on stage as members of Pilate's court. The snare drummer also handles bass drum, the recorder player handles the gong.

The running time is approximately one hour.

Preface

The past few years have seen an enormous resurgence of the religious drama. From the stately pageants of *Herod* and *Daniel* to the highly contemporary *Jesus Christ, Superstar, Godspell,* and, most recently, Leonard Bernstein's *Mass,* we have ample testimony that our modern spirituality is alive and well and living in the theater. It is in light of this growing interest and growing need for performable pieces that I offer the English cycle plays.

The plays, dating from the 14th century, have much in common with the plays already named. Like *Herod* and *Daniel,* they are historical masterpieces, offering both the challenge of scholarly reconstruction and the beauty of medieval ritual and pageantry. With *Superstar, Godspell,* and *Mass* they share a theology that is alive, provocative, and deeply human. In contrast to all the others, however, they offer one great advantage for modern performers: designed originally for amateurs, they come most alive in an amateur production and stay generally within the scope of an amateur undertaking. The text is spoken rather than sung (although music figures prominently), the parts are fairly short and numerous enough to give everyone a chance, and the set and lighting are rudimentary. With a concentrated effort, an enterprising congregation has a reasonable chance of achieving a first-rate performance.

Up to this point the plays have existed only in scholarly versions in Middle English, or in the sketchiest of translations. In preparing a performing edition, I have tried to steer a close course between scholarly accuracy and the demands of actual production. The text has been modernized, but most of its old rhyme scheme and much of its old flavor have been left untouched; notes explain some of the more difficult readings. I have also included a rather lengthy introduction touching on some matters of history and some concrete suggestions for performance. The director is encouraged to use his own imagination.

In their original form, the plays were not liturgically fixed; they can thus be staged at any time of the year. Some connections, though, seem obvious, and it would be hard to imagine the Resurrection play too far removed from the Easter season. We have found that a specific liturgical context adds to the effectiveness of the play: our first performance was part of the Easter Eve Vigil service—on April 1, 1972, at St. Mary's Episcopal Church, Hamilton Village, Philadelphia, Pa.

Cynthia Bourgeault

Philadelphia Divinity School
JULY, 1973

Introduction

I. THE CYCLE DRAMA

By the fourteenth century it had become traditional in many English towns to celebrate the feast of Corpus Christi (the third Thursday after Trinity Sunday, generally late May) with a full-scale series of plays depicting the Biblical history of the world from Creation to Doomsday. Play cycles of this type, sometimes numbering as many as forty-eight plays, are extant from York, Chester, Wakefield, Coventry, and N-Town (an unidentified village), and constitute some of our earliest examples of English vernacular drama.

The circumstances under which these plays were produced are a reflection of that peculiar genius of the Middle Ages, the persistent fusing of sacred and secular. The playwrights are largely anonymous (although a strong clerical hand is suspected), but the moving force behind the productions themselves seems to have been the local businessmen. Individual plays were apportioned to the various town guilds—often with ironic appropriateness, as in *Noah* to the shipbuilders, *The Crucifixion* to the butchers—and were normally staged on huge float-like affairs known as pageant wagons (not unlike the floats in today's parades), which lumbered slowly about the town on a prescribed route from play station to play station. Scrupulous records were kept, generally in the guild ledger books, and from them we can reconstruct much of both the form and flavor of the early plays. The following entry is from York:

Item, to reward to Maisturres grymbesby for lending of her geir ffor pylett's wyfe. Xii d.

The plays enjoyed an enormous popularity and were staged regularly for well over two hundred years, even into the height of the Elizabethan era. It was not until the seventeenth century that the tradition finally died out.

In considering the literary qualities of these plays, we are continually impressed by the variety and boldness of dramatic experimentation. Up to this point church drama had been almost entirely liturgical, relying upon the characteristics of liturgy itself—formality, dignity, Latin rather than English, and a sung rather than spoken dialogue—to create aesthetic unity. With the cycle plays this liturgical context has been abandoned, and the dramatic force comes to rest more and more squarely upon man himself. For the first time man becomes a full-fledged actor in the "play" before God, and with this admission the drama is opened to the full range of human emotion: anger, love, tenderness, joy, laughter, tragedy. Much of the cycle drama is very funny—as, for example in Noah's wife's militant refusal to enter the ark.

In a larger sense, though, these light moments are bound to the darker cruelties of the human condition—the cold and hunger of the shepherds, the pathetic slaughter of the Innocents, the brutal Crucifixion itself—and the darkness is never quite forgotten. It is this unflinching insistence upon all sides of human experience that makes the cycle drama so remarkable. Its dramatic material is the stuff of real life, and through this material the sacred becomes both more accessible and more real.

II. THE WAKEFIELD RESURRECTION PLAY

Among the cycles, Wakefield is remarkable for its dramatic sophistication and the honesty with which it approaches its Biblical characters. These traits are particularly evident in the Resurrection play, harmonizing with the traditional elements of the Easter narrative to create a stunning juxtaposition of human and sacred.

As the play opens, we find Pilate's centurion standing alone, musing over the terrible omens surrounding the death of Christ. Greatly troubled, he resolves to depart at once for Pilate's court to convince them that a mistake has been made. The results are predictable: rude taunts and renewed assertions of Pilate's authority, ending with the centurion's forcible ejection from the court. His message is not without effect, though, for Pilate, afraid that the disciples will steal the body and then claim that it has risen by itself, decides that the tomb must be put under strict surveillance. Four soldiers are summoned: they head off to their posts with inordinate bravado and immediately fall asleep.

Up to this point, a comedy of human errors. With the appearance of Christ, however, we have a moment unequalled anywhere in cycle drama. In contrast to most cycles, in which Christ emerges from his ordeal untouched in either body or spirit and merely resumes his ministry where he left off, we have here a raging, pain-racked human being, nearly broken in spirit, who must first rage and sob and only afterwards can grope his way to a realization of his triumph. His five-minute soliloquy is a remarkable experience, a sort of headlong plunge into the depths of the Christian Mystery, carried off with laser-like intensity.

Afterwards the play returns to its traditional story, but with a continuing emphasis on the human element.

The three Marys enter tearfully, encounter the angels, and conduct their famous dialogue:

> Whom seek ye—ye followers of Christ? . . .
> Why seek ye the living among the dead?
> He is not here, he is risen.

Mary Salome and Mary Jacoby depart joyfully, but Mary Magdalene is not quite consoled and remains behind at the grave, lamenting her loss in terms suspiciously reminiscent of medieval courtly love. Her commotion wakens the guards, and a bit of pure vaudeville ensues as they discover the empty tomb, rapidly pass the buck, and lament the unhappy fate awaiting them. At last they decide that honesty is the only policy, and reminding each other that they "die but once," they skulk off to Pilate. To their enormous surprise, Pilate not only forgives them, but even rewards them handsomely—provided, of course, that they insist everywhere upon the story that an entire army came to steal the body from them. They go off, rejoicing at their good fortune.

The scene returns to the tomb, where Christ, dressed as the gardener, and Mary Magdalene have their final encounter. In most cycles this moment presents insurmountable difficulties, and the usual evasion is to present Christ as pedagogue and Magdalene as his worshipful disciple. In Wakefield, however, a prototype for the transition from human passion to divine love has already been tested in Christ's soliloquy; this same movement now leads us gracefully through the scene with Mary—and with touching credibility.

The Wakefield Resurrection is one of the masterpieces of cycle drama. Despite its highly traditional elements, the resolutions are far from traditional, and its realism, irony, and profound humanity make it of more than ordinary interest to today's audiences. Christ has risen, but at what cost and with what implications? In this play the answers are not automatic: our attention is centered above all upon the awesome reality of the Resurrection itself, and upon a Christ who is both poignant in his humanity and terrifying in his divinity.

III. THE CHARACTERS

Most cycle plays are notoriously lacking in stage directions, and the actual realization of the characters becomes a matter of reading the text sensitively and then using one's imagination. I offer a few suggestions; the director is encouraged to add his own.

PILATE, CAIPHAS, ANNAS.

Throughout the Wakefield cycle, Pilate is consistently characterized as an arch-villain—inhuman, devoid of either compassion or fallibility. The most ominous of the cyclic tyrants, he must at all times convey a pose of absolute authority and menacing foul humor.

In contrast, Caiphas and Annas are pretentious clowns, whose presence in the court scenes inevitably undercuts Pilate's evilness and deflects it into a sort of medieval black humor. Care must be taken to distinguish between the two: Caiphas, the high priest, is pompous, easily ruffled, and easily confused. Annas is cool, slick, and scheming. A political professional, he is the one who invariably comes up with the face-saving scheme, the expedient solution. In our production we emphasized the contrast by adding a physical one: Caiphas was portrayed by a large man with a high, rather squeaky voice; Annas was a tiny man with a deep voice. The Mutt and Jeff effect communicated excellently.

THE CENTURION.

The centurion is a man of God, the first and perhaps the only one in the play to grasp the significance of the miracles revealed. One must avoid the temptation to play him as a simple-hearted or superstitious fool. He is no saint or seer, but rather a stubborn realist, a military man who believes his own eyes and sticks to his belief with a firm, though hopeless, dignity. We must admire in him a sort of desperate courage, and this quality should predominate in portraying him.

THE SOLDIERS.

Upon the soldiers rests the main comic force of the drama, and they can legitimately be played with broad slapstick. Historically, they belong to a common medieval type, the *miles gloriosus,* or boastful soldier, and the humor is one of incongruity—the contrast between their glorious pretensions and their all-too-apparent human failings. To emphasize the former, we added a polished military march from Pilate's court to the sepulchre and a sentry routine at the sepulchre itself. The latter really takes care of itself, requiring only a sensitivity to the soldiers' terror when they must go and confess, and an awareness of their gratitude when Pilate spares them. For real comic effect, they should be played not so much as villains, but as ordinary human beings.

CHRIST.

The role of Christ is an exceedingly difficult one, requiring a highly controlled transition from violent rage to regenerative love. In order for the portrait to be effective, both aspects must be equally real.

THE THREE MARYS.

The Marys are the only female element in the play, and their appearance immediately after Christ's exit brings a broadening and softening of the emotional tonalities. Up to this point, except for Christ, we have had only boasting, threats, and anger: the Marys bring weeping, tenderness, and joy. This female color should be stressed, particularly in Mary Salome and Mary Jacoby, who remain otherwise undifferentiated.

Mary Magdalene is a character almost as complex as Christ and requiring the same interaction of human passion and divine love. For most of the play, her characterization is strongly reminiscent of medieval courtly love, in which hero worship and sexuality are hopelessly intertwined, and one suspects that for her the triumph of the Resurrection is overshadowed by the immensity of her personal loss—this aspect, anyway, must be emphasized in her tomb soliloquy. In the final scene between her and Christ the movement is one of gentle release, from human to spiritual love, but even here we may suspect that she misses the point, for her final song is mostly adolescent rapture:

> My bliss is come, my care is gone,
> my lovely one I've met alone . . .

All three Marys move with dignity and decorum and are granted the rank of fine ladies, true and pious believers.

THE ANGELS.

The angels must be dignified, but also strange and fiery. There is mystery and terror in Christ's emergence from the tomb; these feelings must be conveyed. We had them speak in deep, slow voices and maintain a sentry-like stiffness in their watch over the tomb.

IV. SET AND LIGHTING

Simplicity should be the key. Whether in the church or on a pageant wagon, medieval drama always operated within a severely restricted playing area and used the most rudimentary of props. Our production, designed for a church sanctuary, relied upon two very basic "sets"—the sepulchre and Pilate's court, which were placed at stage center and stage right in the front of the church. The sepulchre, our most ambitious building project, consisted of a large "box," six feet high and approximately two feet deep, partially open at the back, and sturdy enough to allow the two angels to stand on top. Two smaller platforms were added at the three-foot level, and steps led up from behind so that the angels could mount easily during the Resurrection sequence. The front of the sepulchre was fashioned from two iron gates (we found them in the church basement), which were hinged to swing open easily. A chair was provided within the tomb for Christ to sit on, out of sight, and he entered the tomb early—about a half hour before show time.

Pilate's court was extremely simple, consisting of a slightly elevated platform upon which were placed chairs for Caiphas and Annas, and a higher platform, immediately adjacent to it and connected by steps, which contained Pilate's throne. To add an element of pageantry, we included a few flagstands and banners.

In staging the play, we relied considerably on the medieval concept of "place" to facilitate entrances and exits. In simplest terms, this amounts to a series of movable scenes, in which the actors, who have entered at the beginning of the play and taken their seats in assigned positions, merely move from their own position to somebody else's to create an encounter. Thus, there is no need for Pilate and his court to move "offstage" when the scene shifts to the sepulchre; the fact that they are not speaking constitutes an automatic offstage, and no inconsistency is felt in their continued physical presence. This artifice is standard procedure in medieval drama and should present no problems for today's audiences.

If the play is being staged in a church, it is a good idea to use the whole church as a playing area. We achieved some excellent results by playing Christ's soliloquy in the center aisle of the nave, moving gradually towards the back of the church and exiting by that back door. This procedure also allows a more immediate involvement of the audience, particularly if Christ singles out individuals in the audience to whom he can direct his diatribe. Similarly, the soldiers' march to the tomb started at the back of the center aisle, and the march reverberated the whole length of the church. The recessional, of course, must use this center aisle and side aisles too, if they are available.

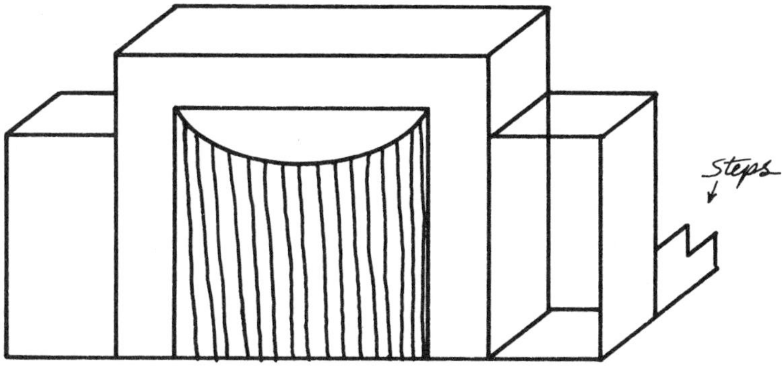

Figure 1 The Sepulchre – Front & Side

Figure 2 The playing area (sample)

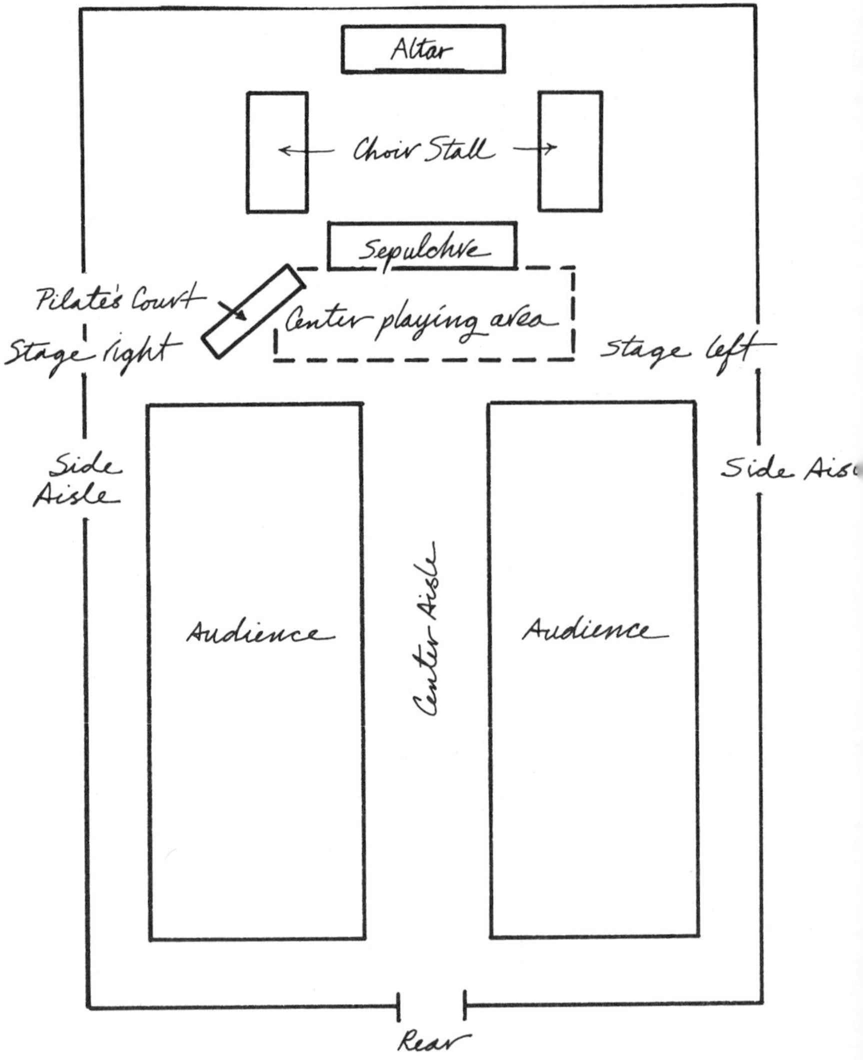

As for lighting, simplicity should again prevail. We used two white theater spotlights, one on Pilate's court and one on the sepulchre. The normal overhead lights in the sanctuary were replaced with 75-watt red floodlights, and we did take the liberty of playing the resurrection sequence and Christ's soliloquy in red—an eerie effect. Normal lighting was restored after Christ's exit.

Candles may be used very effectively. We equipped all the angels with torches and added candlelight to the resurrection and the recessional. If the play is produced as part of an Easter Vigil service, a fine touch can be had by lighting the angels' candles from the Paschal candle at the beginning of the performance.

A small rheostat dimmer box is useful, particularly in the first scene with the centurion and in the tomb scene as the soldiers gradually fall asleep.

V. COSTUMES

It has been convincingly proven that costumes in medieval plays were medieval, and not reproductions of Biblical styles. Thus, cycle kings and dignitaries are medieval kings and dignitaries, musicians are minstrels, soldiers are knights, women are courtly (or peasant) ladies. In designing costumes, one can profitably consult reproductions of medieval art, particularly stained glass windows.

In our production we created an additional effect by clothing the evil characters—Pilate, Caiphas, and Annas—in ridiculous finery and the good characters—the centurion and the Marys—in rather plain and drab outfits symbolic of their mourning. The angels, of course, must be formal and impressive. Details are given below:

PILATE, CAIPHAS, ANNAS: full length robes of a rich and rather heavy material. We clad Pilate in gold, Caiphas in lavender, and Annas in turquoise. Caiphas wore a bishop's mitre, Pilate a heavy crown. All were bearded.

THE CENTURION: a dark tunic and tights, heavy boots, gloves, a shield.

THE SOLDIERS: more colorful tunics and tights, boots, gloves. All four carry large spears.

CHRIST: a rag, torn and shredded, the remains of his burial linens. We smeared him with mud and ashes, mussed his hair, and drew bruises and cuts on his body.

THE MARYS: rather pretty and colorful dresses of courtly style, covered in the early part of the play by long, drab mourning capes. The Marys carry small flasks of oil to annoint the body.

THE ANGELS: the two speaking angels were dressed in long robes of white damask with long gold streamers flowing from the sleeves. The angel choir wore long robes of rather shiny material (dress lining) in colors of fire–pink, orange, red, gold. The children wore white. All angels were in stocking feet.

THE PAGES AND MUSICIANS: tights and tunics in colors complementing those of Pilate's court.

VI. THE MUSIC

The problem of music in the cycle plays is still under considerable investigation. Generally speaking, singing seems to have played a relatively minor role, limited normally to the angels and the shepherds, and then only for special occasions. Where singing is called for, it is almost invariably monophonic and in Latin—in other words, neither folk song nor polyphony seem to find their way into the repertoire. Similarly, instrumental music is infrequently called for, except in occasional processionals and interludes. One must remember that the cycle plays are dramas and not operettas, and any music that is added must be done tastefully and within the spirit of the play.

In *The Wakefield Resurrection Play* music is referred to twice. A "Te Deum" recessional is specifically called for, and some sort of angelic singing is strongly suggested in the second soldier's report to Pilate, "We heard never in evening or morn . . . such melody." For this music we supplied the famous "Alle Psallite cum Luya," a 13th century motet from Worcester Cathedral. Some may be familiar with it from the New York Pro Musica's restoration of the liturgical play of Herod. The text runs as follows: "Let us sing to the lord Alleluya; let us sing heartily to the lord Alleluya; let us with hearts totally devoted to the lord sing Alleluya."

In addition to these passages, singing was added in two other places. Since the play was performed apart from its cyclic context, a musical introduction seemed appropriate: the children sang a two-voice prayer, "Rex Coeli Domine." The text is "King of the Heavens, Lord of the wave-sounding sea, Of the shining sun and the squalid earth, Thy humble servants, venerating Thee with pious accents entreat that Thou wilt order them freed from manifold ills."

After Christ's exit a choral commentary seemed similarly appropriate. We chose a 15th century motet by Jacob Obrecht, "Parce, Domine": "Have mercy, O Lord, on thy people, for Thou art kind and merciful. Hear us forever, O Lord."

A few instrumental touches were added to the Pilate scenes—a drum roll to occasion Pilate's first entrance, a medieval march "L'Homme Armé" ("the armed man") to accompany the soldiers to the sepulchre. In the "Alle Psallite," the organ doubled the entire song the last time through, and the bass drum accompanied throughout.

With regard to the handbells, which are heard in the "Rex Coeli" and the "Te Deum," we distributed them to members of the cast, who stationed them offstage or under their seats onstage as follows:

C_4 : Caiphas, under his seat
G_4 : Angel 1, in the sepulchre
C_5 : Mary Salome, in her seat offstage
E_5 : Soldier 2, in his seat offstage
G_5 : Mary Jacoby, in her seat offstage
A_5 : Annas, under his seat
C_6 : Angel 2, in the sepulchre.

A Suggested Bibliography

Anderson, M. D. *Drama and Imagery in English Medieval Churches.* Cambridge, Cambridge University Press, 1963.

Chambers, E. K. *The Mediaeval Stage.* 2 volumes. Oxford, Oxford University Press, 1903.

Collins, Fletcher. *The Production of Medieval Church Drama.* Charlottesville, Va., University of Virginia Press, 1972.

Hardison, O. B. *Christian Rite and Christian Drama in the Middle Ages.* Baltimore, Johns Hopkins Press, 1965.

Kinghorn, A. M. *Medieval Drama.* London, Evans Brothers, Ltd., 1968.

Kolve, V. A. *A Play Called Corpus Christi.* Palto Alto, Cal., Stanford University Press, 1972.

Williams, Arnold. *The Character of Pilate in the Towneley Plays.* East Lansing, Mich., Michigan State University Press, 1950.

ACKNOWLEDGMENTS

The Towneley Plays. Ed. George England. New York, Oxford University Press, 1966; reprint.

Masterpieces of Music before 1750. Carl Parrish and John F. Ohl. New York, Norton, 1951.

Historical Anthology of Music. 2 volumes. Volume 1: Oriental, Medieval, and Renaissance Music, 1949. Volume 2: Baroque, Rococo, and Pre-Classical Music, 1950. Eds. Archibald T. Davison and Willi Apel. Cambridge, Mass., Harvard University Press.

The Wakefield Resurrection Play

In the dark, the ANGELS *enter silently and file into the choir stalls. The actors take up positions offstage:* PILATE, CAIPHAS, ANNAS, SOLDIERS, *pages, musicians stage right; the* MARYS *stage left.*

The CENTURION *stands in the middle of the stage, immediately before the sepulchre.*

The C_5 handbell sounds three long notes.

The children sing:

[Music 1 "Rex Coeli, Domine"]

The handbell E_5 sounds once.

The lights gradually rise on the CENTURION.

CENTURION:
Ah, blessed Lord, Adonai![1]
What may this marvel signify
that here was shown so openly
unto our sight,
When that righteous man can die
that Jesus hight?[2]

Heaven it shook abone,[3]
of shining ceased both sun and moon,
and dead men also rose up soon
out of their grave;

1. *Adonai*—praised be ye
2. *hight (hite)*—to be called
3. *abone*—violently

and stones in the wall anon
in sunder burst and clave.[4]

There was seen full many a solemn sight;
our princes, forsooth, did nothing right![5]
And so I said to them on height
as it is true:
that he was most of might,
the son of God, Jesu.

Fowls in the air and fish in the flood
that day changed their mood
when he was rent upon the rood,[6]
that lord, I say;
full well *they* understood
that he was slain that day.

Therefore, right as I may
to them fast will I ride,
to learn without delay
what they will say this tide
of this affair.
I will no longer abide,
but part at once for there.

He exits down the center aisle. The light fades on the sepulchre and rises on Pilate's court. The musicians and flagbearers are on stage. A drum roll signals the entrance, stage right, of PILATE, *followed by* CAIPHAS *and* ANNAS.

PILATE:
Peace I warn you, guard your wit!
and stand aside, or else go sit;
for here are men that go not yet,
and lords of greatest might.

4. *clave*—to break in half 5. *forsooth*—truly 6. *rent upon the rood*—torn apart on the cross

We mean to abide and not to flit,
    I tell you every wight.[7]

Spare your speech, you boasters bold,
and cease your cry till I have told
those things that my worship will
here in these wones;[8]
whosoever ventures ill,
    full high be hanged his bones!

He sits down on his throne. As soon as he is seated, CAIPHAS *and* ANNAS *sit. The flagbearers plant their flags and exit.*

PILATE (*continuing*):
Know ye not that I am Pilate,
that sat upon the judgment of late
at Calvary, where I was at
this day at morn?
I am he, that great state,
    that lad has all to-torn.[9]

Now, since that loathly louse is dead,
I have great joy in my manhood;
therefore, may it in this stead[10]
    be henceforth taken heed,
if any follow what he said,
    or more his law would lead.

For if I know it, cruelly
his life is lost—and that full shortly!
for he is better hung full high
    on gallow tree;

7. *wight (wite)*—person
8. *wones*—places
9. *that lad has all to-torn*—that has torn that lad all apart
10. *stead*—place

(*to* CAIPHAS *and* ANNAS)
therefore ye prelates should a-spy
if any such be.

As I am a man of power most,
if there be any that make such boast,
with torments keen shall he be lost
for evermore;
the devil to hell shall harry his ghost—
but I say no more.

CAIPHAS:
Sir, of that be not adread,
for Centurio, I understand,
your knight, is in that stead
right there behind.
We left him there as man most wise,
should any rebels try to rise—
to seize them to the next Assize
and then for to make end.

The CENTURION *enters, stage right.*

CENTURION:
God save you sirs, on every side!
Worship and wealth in world so wide!

PILATE:
Centurio, welcome this tide,
our comely knight![11]

CENTURION (*coldly*):
God grant that grace will foreto guide[12]
and rule you right!

11. *comely (cumly)*—fine, esteemed

12. *foreto*—henceforth

PILATE:
Centurio, welcome, draw near at hand!
Tell us some tidings here among,
for you have gone throughout our land—
you know full well . . .

CENTURION:
Sir, I dread me ye have done wrong,
and wonder ill.

CAIPHAS (*scornfully*):
Wonder ill? I pray thee, why?
Declare that to this company!

CENTURION:
So shall I, sir, full certainly,
with all my main:
that righteous man, as all can see,
you had him slain.

PILATE:
Centurio, cease of such talk!
Ye are a great man of our law,
and if a witness we should draw
to us excuse,
to maintain us evermore ye shall,
and *not refuse.*

CENTURION:
To maintain truth is more worthy.
I said when I saw him die
that it was God's son almighty
that hung there—
I say and yet abide thereby
for evermore.

ANNAS:
Yea, sir, such ravings may ye rue!
Thou should not warble such notes new.
But if you know some tokens true,
unto us tell.

CENTURION:
Such wondrous things never ere ye knew
as then befell.

CAIPHAS:
We pray thee tell us, of what things?

CENTURION:
Of elements, both old and young,
in their manner made great mourning
in that stead:
they knew by countenance that their king
was done to dead.

The sun for woe it waxed all wan,
the moon and stars, of shining gone,
and earth it trembled, as a man
afraid to speak;
the stone that never stirred 'ere then
in sunder burst and broke,

and dead men rose up bodily, both great and small . . .

PILATE (*sarcastically*):
Centurio, beware withall!
Eclipse is what the learned call
this solemn sight,
that sun and moon in some seasons
lack of their light.

CAIPHAS:
Sir, and if that dead men rise up bodily,

that may be done through sorcery;
therefore nothing we set thereby
    that you tell us.

CENTURION:
Sir, what I truly saw,
    that shall I evermore trust.

Not for the work that ye did work,
not only that the sun grew dark,
but how the veil tore in the church,
    that I'd like to know!

PILATE:
Ah, such tales full soon will make us irked
    if they are told!

Harlot! why have you thus come us among,
with such bold lies us to confound?
Wend forth! High might thou hang,
    vile traitor!

CAIPHAS:
Wend forth in the courtyard
    and hold still thy clatter!

CENTURION:
Sirs, since ye set not by my words,
    have now good day.
God grant you grace to know
    the truth all the way.

He leaves. ANNAS, *following him to the edge of the playing area, shouts after him:*

ANNAS:
Withdraw thee fast, since that thou dreads,
for we shall well maintain our deeds!

PILATE:
Such wondrous tidings as he now reads[13]
were never before!

CAIPHAS:
To warble this note no more we need,
neither evening nor morn!

But still, I find cause for alarm,
that afterwards might do us harm;
therefore, sir, while you are here
among us all,
advise us of these tokens sore,
how they will stand.

For Jesus said full openly
unto the men that passed him by
a thing that grieves all Jewry,
and might so may:
that he should rise up bodily
within the third day.

If it be so, as I have said,
this latter deed is more to dread
than is the first, if we take heed
and tend thereto:
Advise us, sir, for it is need
the best to do.

ANNAS (*to* CAIPHAS, *scornfully*):
Sir, even if he promised so,
he has no might to rise and go . . .
But . . . his disciples steal his corpse from us,
and home it bear,
t'would be for us and others more
a foul affair.

13. *wondrous*—strange

Then would the people say, every one,
that he were risen himself alone;
therefore, ordain to keep that stone
    with soldiers' hand
till these three days be come and gone
    and brought to end.

PILATE:
Now truly, sir, full well you say;
and for this one point to purvey[14]
I shall, if that I may:
    He shall not rise!
Nor none shall win him thence away
    in any wise.

At a signal from PILATE *the drummer sounds a roll. The* SOLDIERS *enter stage right, marching in single file. Upon command of the* FIRST SOLDIER *they draw to attention and salute in unison.*

PILATE:
Sir knights, that are of deeds most true,
and chosen chiefly for chivalry,
as I may thus depend on you
    by day and night,
ye go and keep Jesu's body
    with all your might.

And whatever else ye do,
keep him well unto the third day,
that no traitor steal his corpse from you
    out of that stead;
for if they do, truly I say,
    ye shall be dead.

14. *purvey*—to oversee, superintend

FIRST SOLDIER:
Yes, Sir Pilate, in certain
we shall keep him with all our main;
there shall no traitor with no pain
  steal him from us.
Sir knights, take gear that best may gain
  and let us go!

SECOND SOLDIER:
Yea, truly we are ready bound!
We shall keep him for your renown;
On every side let us sit down
  without a fear—
and I shall fain to crack his crown
  who comes here!

Upon command of the FIRST SOLDIER, *they salute again, turn, and exit in a march. The drummer and recorder player accompany them a few steps behind, playing the following tune:*

[Music 2 "L'Homme Armé"]

The march to the sepulchre should be clearly audible, and if possible, clearly visible.

When they reach the sepulchre, the SOLDIERS *draw into a strict military formation and do a salute with their spears. Afterwards, they fall "at ease," and the musicians exit, stage left.*

FIRST SOLDIER:
Who should be where, fain would I wit?[15]

SECOND SOLDIER:
Even on this side will I sit!

THIRD SOLDIER:
And I shall forbid his feet to flit.

FOURTH SOLDIER:
He goes nowhere!
Now by Mohammed, fain would I wit
who dares come here,
this corpse with treason for to take:

for if it were a burning drake,[16]
from me stiffly he'd get a stroke,
have here my glove!
Till these three days be past,
this body shall not move!

The SOLDIERS *take up their positions as follows:*

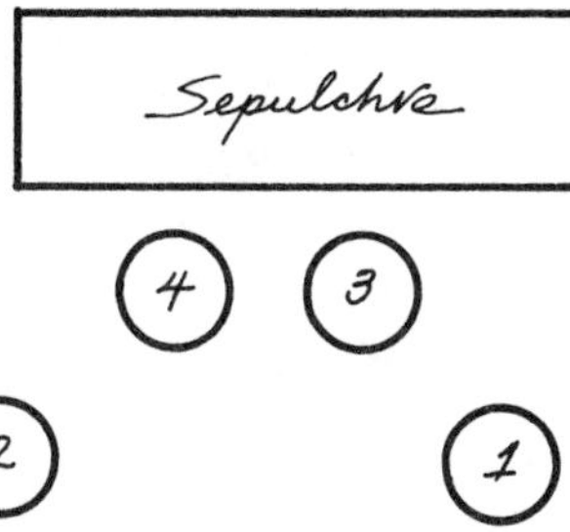

FIRST SOLDIER *and* SECOND SOLDIER *stand downstage at attention. They gradually relax their attention and fall asleep.*

THIRD SOLDIER *and* FOURTH SOLDIER *begin a sentry tour of duty before the tomb: three steps apart, about face, three steps together. The military bravado should be exaggerated. After three complete tours, the* FOURTH SOLDIER *takes his three steps apart, notices the others seated, and sits down himself. The* THIRD SOLDIER, *standing alone, completes*

15. *wit*—know or see 16. *drake*—dragon

another round of marching, then shrugs his shoulders, sits down, and falls asleep.

During this last sequence the stage lights should gradually be dimming, and the bass drum begins, slowly and rhythmically. As the THIRD SOLDIER *falls asleep, the red lights come up, and the* Alle psallite cum luya *begins:*

[Music 3 "Alle psallite cum luya"]

The song is sung by the ANGELS, *both adults and children. As they sing, they should move forward in two files onto the stage. Their route should lead them through the tomb and onto the center playing area where the* SOLDIERS *are asleep. The two speaking* ANGELS *bring up the rear of the processional, and at the end of the song they mount to the top of the sepulchre.*

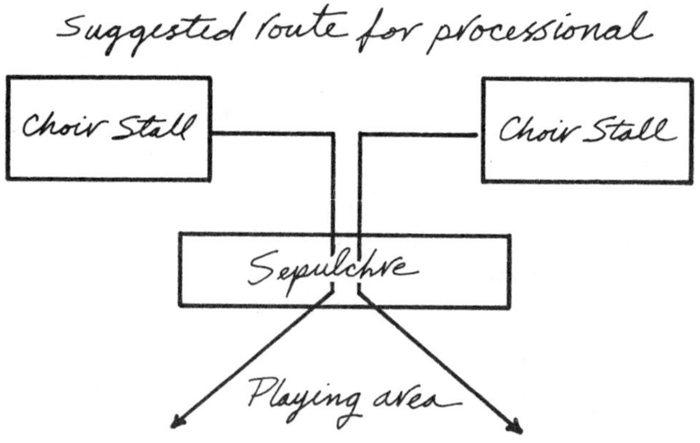

When all ANGELS *have entered and the song is ended, from the tomb comes a groan.* CHRIST *emerges slowly and painfully. He surveys the audience in silence and slowly begins his speech.*

At the sound of the groan, the CHILD ANGELS *scream and scatter offstage. The* ADULTS *remain, solid and immobile.*

CHRIST:
Earthly man that I have wrought,
boldly wake, and sleep thou nought!
With bitter bale I have thee bought
to make thee free;
into this dungeon deep I sought,
and all for love of thee.

Behold how dear I would thee buy:
my wounds are wet and all bloody;
thee, sinful man, full dear bought I
with torments keen;
defile thee not again thereby—
now art thou clean.

Clean have I made thee, sinful man;
with woe and weeping I thee won;
from heart and side the blood out ran—
such was my pain—
thou must love me, who thereby gave
my life for thine.

Thou, sinful man, that on me gaze,
tight unto me thou turn thy face!
Behold my body in this place,
how it was dight—[17]
all to-rent and all to-shent[18]
man, for thy plight!

Behold my shanks and my knees,[19]
my arms and my thighs;
behold me well, look what thou sees:

17. *dight (dite)*—injured
18. *all to-rent and all to-shent*—all beaten and torn

but sorrow and pain—
thus was I spilt, man, for *thy* guilt,
and not for mine.

Behold my body, how Jews it dang,[20]
with knots of whips and scourges stang—
like streams from a well the blood out sprang
on every side—
knots where they hit, well may thou wit,
made wounds wide.

And therefore, thou shalt understand—
in body, head, feet, and hand
four hundred wounds and five thousand
here may thou see:
and of them, all were dealt full well
for love of thee.

Behold of me nought else is left . . .

He pauses for a moment, then sinks to the floor.

But 'ere that thou were from me reft,
all these pains would I suffer again
and for thee die;
here may thou see that I love thee
man, faithfully.

Since I for love, man, bought thee dear,
as thou thyself can well see here,
I pray thee heartily, with good cheer[21]
love me again;
for it *pleased* me that I for thee
bore all this pain.

If thou thy life in sin have led,
mercy to ask be not adread;

19. *shanks*—calves **20.** *dang*—beat

the slightest drop I for thee bled
 might cleanse thee soon—
all the sin, the world within[22]
 If thou had done.

I was well wroth with Judas,[23]
that he would not ask me for grace
when it was for *his* trespass
 that he me sold;
I was ready to show mercy;
 ask none he would.

Lo how I hold my arms out wide,
thee to save, all ready-made;
the endless love I for thee had
 well may thou know—
some love again I would full fain
 thou would me show.

But love nought else, I ask of thee,
and that thou hold fast, sin to flee;
pain thee to live in charity
 both night and day,
then in my bliss that never shall miss
 thou shalt dwell ay.[24]

For I am the veray prince of peace,[25]
and bitter sins I may release;
and whoso will of sins cease
 and mercy cry,
I grant them here a mass,
 in bread, my own body!

21. *cheer*—courage
22. *all the sin, the world within*—all the sin in the world
23. *wroth*—angry
24. *ay*—forever 25. *veray*—true

Christ exits.

It is effective to play this scene in the center aisle, moving gradually to the back. If side aisles are available, the ANGELS *should gradually spread into them, following Christ's movement. After his exit, they draw together in the back to sing. If no side aisles are available, they can remain in position at the front of the church.*

[Music 4 "Parce, Domine"]

At the end of the song the ANGELS *exit. As the* ANGELS *leave, the red lights fade and the normal spotlight comes up again on the sepulchre. The* MARYS *enter, stage left, weeping. As they talk, they move slowly towards stage center.*

MAGDALENE:
Alas! to die with dole am I dight![25a]
In world was never a woefuller wight;
I drop, I dare, for sighing of sight[26]
  that I can see;
my lord, that greatest was of might,
  is dead from me.

M. JACOBY:
Alas! how stand I on my feet
when I think of his wounds wet?
Jesus, that was in love so sweet
  and never did ill
is dead and graven under the grate
  for no cause at all.

M. SALOME:
Without a cause these Jews each one
that lovely lord they have him slain;

25a. *dight (dite)*—fated   26. *I dare*—I dare say

and trespass did he never none
 in any stead;
to whom shall we make our moan?
 our lord is dead!

They weep again, more vehemently.

MAGDALENE:
Since he is dead, my sisters dear,
wend we will with full good cheer[27]
with our annointments fair and clear
 that we have brought,
for to annoint his bitter wounds
 that the Jews have wrought.

M. JACOBY:
Come, my sisters, then with me,
for sore I long his corpse to see;
but I know never what best may be,
 help have we none;
and which of us three women
 shall remove the stone?

M. SALOME:
That do we not, unless we were more,
for it is high and heavy also.

MAGDALENE:
Sisters, we shall never move that door,
 nor make mourning . . .

They start to exit stage right, sadly, heads down. As they pass in front of the sepulchre, something catches Mary Magdalene's attention.

MAGDALENE:
I see two where we wend to
 in white clothing . . .

27. *full good cheer*—stout heart

M. JACOBY:
Indeed, the truth is not to hide—
the grave stone is put aside!

M. SALOME:
Truly, whatever may betide,
    now will we wend
to bear the love, and with him bide
    that was our friend.

They approach the sepulchre.

FIRST ANGEL:
Ye mourning women in your thought,
here in this place, whom have ye sought?

MAGDALENE (*awed*):
Jesus, that unto death was brought,
    our lord so free!

SECOND ANGEL:
Behold, woman, here is he nought—
    come near and see!

FIRST ANGEL:
He is not here, the truth to say—
the place is empty where he lay;
the sudary here, as see you may,[28]
    was on him laid;
he is risen and gone his way—
    as he said.

MARY SALOME *and* MARY JACOBY *enter the tomb cautiously, look around, and then, in growing joy, drop off their mourning capes and embrace each other.* MARY MAGDALENE *stands downstage and to the right of them. She does not enter the tomb.*

SECOND ANGEL:
Even as he said, so done has he:
he is risen through his majesty
and shall be found in Galilee
    in flesh and fell;[29]
to his disciples now wend ye
    and *thus* them tell.

MAGDALENE:
My sisters fair, since it is so
that he is risen from death's woe,
as said to us these angels two,
    our lord and liege,
as ye have heard, where that ye go,
    look that ye preach.

M. JACOBY:
As we have heard, so shall we say;
Mary, our sister, have good day!

MAGDALENE:
Now veray God, as he well may,
    man most of might,
wish you sisters well in your way,
    and rule you right!

MARY JACOBY *and* MARY SALOME *exit, stage left. As soon as they are gone,* MARY MAGDALENE *returns to the sepulchre and weeps bitterly.*

MAGDALENE:
Alas, what shall become of me?
My wretched heart will break in three
when I think of that body,
    how it was spilt;
through feet and hands nailed was he
    without a guilt.

28. *sudary*—shroud   29. *in flesh and fell*—in the flesh

Without a guilt then was he taken;
my lovely lord they have him slain,
and trespass did he never none,
    nor yet no miss;[30]
for *my* guilt was he forfeited,
    and nothing his.

How might I, if I loved that sweet
that for me suffered wounds wet,
except to be buried under the grate
    and end *my* life?
There is nothing till that we meet
    may make me blithe.

Weeping, she moves off to the right and sits down near the FIRST SOLDIER. *Her robe brushes him as she passes. He yawns, stretches, and lumbers to his feet. Suddenly he notices the sepulchre gates standing ajar. He rushes up in shock and horror, ascertains that the sepulchre is really empty, and exclaims:*

FIRST SOLDIER:
Out! Alas; What shall I say?
Where is the corpse that herein lay?

His noise wakens the SECOND SOLDIER, *who stretches ill-humoredly.*

SECOND SOLDIER:
What ails the man?

FIRST SOLDIER:
He is gone that we should tend!
Rise up and see!

30. *miss*—misdeed

SECOND SOLDIER:
Harrow! Thief! For ay I count us shent![31]

The THIRD SOLDIER *awakens.*

THIRD SOLDIER:
What devil ails you two,
such noise and cry thus for to make?

SECOND SOLDIER:
For he is gone!

THIRD SOLDIER:
Alas, who?

SECOND SOLDIER:
He that here lay!

THIRD SOLDIER:
Alas, how did he get away?

FIRST SOLDIER:
Alas, what shall I do this day
since this traitor is gone away?
And safely, sirs, I dare well say
    he rose alone.

SECOND SOLDIER:
If Sir Pilate learns of this affair,
    we are all gone.

The THIRD SOLDIER *pokes the* FOURTH SOLDIER *with his spear, and he, too, awakes.*

FOURTH SOLDIER:
Are you sure he rose in death?

SECOND SOLDIER:
I saw myself, when that he left!

31. *shent*—lost

FIRST SOLDIER:
When that he stirred out of this stead
    none could have known.

FOURTH SOLDIER:
Alas, hard hap is on my head[32]
    among all men!

THIRD SOLDIER:
Yea, if Sir Pilate learns of this deed,
that we were sleeping when he left,
we shall forfeit, take ye heed,
    all that we have.

FOURTH SOLDIER:
We must find some tale, that is clear,
    ourselves to save.

FIRST SOLDIER:
I find that well, before we go!

SECOND SOLDIER:
And I assent to that also!

THIRD SOLDIER:
A thousand, shall I say, and more,
all armed with spear and chain,
came and took his corpse from us—
    had us nearly slain!

FOURTH SOLDIER:
Nay, indeed I hold there none so good
as to tell the truth, right as it stood;
how that he rose with might and main
    and went his way,
to Sir Pilate, if he be wroth,
    thus will I say.

32. *hard hap*—bad luck

FIRST SOLDIER (*amazed*):
Why, and dare you to Sir Pilate go
with these tidings, and tell him so?

SECOND SOLDIER:
So say I that we do also—
we die but once!

ALL SOLDIERS (*in unison, stamping their feet on the second* woe):

Now he that wrought us all this woe,
woe be his bones!

The SOLDIERS *exit, stage center, for Pilate's court, running head-over-heels with no trace of their former admirable decorum. They enter the court stage right and huddle at the entrance, football style, to receive final instructions from the* FIRST SOLDIER.

FIRST SOLDIER:
Now, and I shall tell the words to end,
just as it was . . .

He moves forward, summoning his courage. The others form a line directly behind him.

FIRST SOLDIER:
Sir Pilate, prince without a peer,
Sir Caiphas and Annas, most revered,
and all the knights about you here
to call by name,
Mohammed save you in sorest woe
from sin and shame.

PILATE:
Ye are welcome, our knights so keen,
A mirthful meeting may now be seen.
But tell us some things, us between,
how ye have wrought . . .

FIRST SOLDIER:
Our walking, lord, without a doubt,
is worth to nought.

CAIPHAS:
To nought? Alas, cease of such talk!

SECOND SOLDIER:
The prophet Jesus, that ye well know,
is risen and from us did go
with main and might.

PILATE:
Therefore, the devil keep you all,
vile, worthless knights!
What, churly cowards I you call:
you let him pass from you *all?*

THIRD SOLDIER:
Sir, there was none could do but small
when that he left.

FOURTH SOLDIER:
We were so scared, we all fell down
and quoke for dread.

They all fall to their knees in demonstration.

FIRST SOLDIER:
We were so frightened, everyone,
when that he put aside the stone,
we quoke for fear and dared stir none,
and sore we were oppressed.

PILATE:
Why, rose he by himself alone?

SECOND SOLDIER:
Yea, Sir, of that ye trust.

We heard never in evening or morn,
nor yet our fathers us before,
such melody—midday or morn—
    as was heard there.

PILATE:
Alas, then is our law forlorn[33]
    for evermore.

Ah, devil, what shall now come of this?
The world begins to fare amiss—
I pray ye, Caiphas, ye advise us
    in this affair.

CAIPHAS:
Sir, if I knew ought by my reckonings,
    fain would I say.

ANNAS *rises from his seat, scratching his chin.*

ANNAS:
To say the best indeed *I* shall:
it shall be profit for us all.
It behooves yon knights their words to recall—
    how he is missed;
we would not, for thing that might befall,
    that any man wist.[34]

And therefore, of your courtesy,
    give them a reward thereby.

PILATE *is at first puzzled. Then the light slowly dawns. He pats* ANNAS *on the back.*

PILATE:
With this counsel well pleased am I;
    it shall be thus.

33. *forlorn*—lost   34. *wist*—knew

Sir knights, that are of deeds most high,
 take heed to us.

The soldiers raise their heads cautiously, then slowly rise.

Hearken now how ye shall say
where so ye go by night or day:
ten thousand men of good array
 came you until,[35]
and thievishly took his corpse away
 against your will.

Look that ye say this in every land,
and thereto, on this command,
ten thousand pounds have in your hand
 as your reward.
And my friendship, you understand,
 shall not be spared.

The SOLDIERS *look at each other in disbelief, then suddenly break ranks, slap each others' backs, and dance around for joy. The celebration ends abruptly with Pilate's next command:*

PILATE:
But look that ye say as we have told!

FIRST SOLDIER:
Yes Sir, as Mohammed makes bold,
in every country where we wend
 by night or day,
where so we go, where so we bend,
 thus shall we say.

PILATE:
The blessing of Mohammed be with you night and day!

35. *came you until*—came unto you

Upon command from the FIRST SOLDIER, *they all salute and march out. The recorder player and drummer may reprise the* L'Homme Armé *tune.*

[Music 2 "L'Homme Armé"]

The lights fade on Pilate's court, and the scene shifts back to the sepulchre.

CHRIST *emerges, stage left, still clad in rags. He stands silently by the sepulchre. Then, as if by inspiration, he suddenly picks up Mary Salome's mourning cape and puts it on. He spits on his hands and attempts to wash his face.*

MARY MAGDALENE *looks up, sees him, and runs over to him.*

MAGDALENE:
Say to me, gardener, I thee pray,
if thou bore ought my lord away.
Tell me the truth, say me not nay,
where that he lies,
and I shall remove him if I may
in any wise.

CHRIST (*surly*):
Woman, why weeps thou? Be still!
Whom seeks thou? Tell me thy will,
and nag me not with nay.

MAGDALENE:
For my lord I long full ill:
the place they bore his body to,
tell me, I thee pray;
and I shall, if I may,
his body bear with me
unto my dying day—
the better I should be.

CHRIST:
Woman, woman, turn thy thought!
Wit thou well *I* hid him nought,
nor bore him ought with me.
Go seek: look if thou find him ought!

MAGDALENE:
In faith, I have him sought,
but never found will he be.

CHRIST (*softening*):
Why, what was he to thee, the truth to tell?

MAGDALENE:
He was to me . . . Ah . . . no longer may I dwell . . .

CHRIST (*gently*):
Mary, thou seeks thy God, and I am he.

MAGDALENE:
Rabony, my lord so dear![36]
Now am I whole, that thou art here!
Suffer me to draw thee near and kiss thy feet—
might I do so, well would I be, for thou art sweet!

She falls in ecstasy at his feet.

CHRIST:
Nay, Mary, touch not me,
for to my Father, I tell thee,
have I not yet talked.
Tell my brothers I shall be
before them all in Trinity,
whose will that I have wrought.

To peace now are they brought
that previous were in pain;
wherefore now thank in thought
God, thy lord and mine.

36. *Rabony*—Hebrew for *my Lord*

Mary, thou shalt wend from me—
on my errand thou shalt gratefully go—
    in no floundering thou fall—
to my disciples say thou so
that now are wretched and lapped in woe,
    that succor them I shall.

By name Peter thou call,
and say that I shall be
before him and them all,
myself, in Galilee.

He starts to leave, then turns back and kisses her gently on the forehead. He exits, stage right.

MAGDALENE:
Lord, I shall make my voyage
to tell them hastily;
when they hear that message,
they will all be merry.

This lord was slain, alas thereby,
falsely spilt, no one knew why,
    where he did miss.
But with him I spoke boldly,
    therefore is come my bliss!

My bliss is come, my care is gone,
my lovely one I've met alone!
I am as blithe in blood and bone
    as ever was wight!
Now is he risen that was slain:
    my heart is light.

She dances around joyfully.

I am as light as leaf on tree
for joyful sight that I can see!
Full well I know that it was he, my Lord Jesu.

He who betrayed that free, sore may he rue.[37]

To Galilee now will I fare
and his disciples fetch from care.
I know that they will mourn no more;
now is come their bliss!
That worthy child that Mary bore,
may he amend *your* miss!

The lights darken. After two tolls on the E_5 *bell, the* Te Deum *chant begins offstage.*

[Music 5 "Te Deum"]

On the word Sanctus *the choir moves into the church, carrying candles. Members of the cast holding handbells add them, one by one, to the melody.*

A suggested route for the recessional in a church containing side aisles is: enter from rear, proceed up side aisles in two columns to the playing area.

At the sepulchre the two columns come together to process double-file down the center aisle. As the procession passes various members of the cast, they fall into place in the line, interspersed among the singers.

In a church without side aisles an alternate route can be found. The chant should time out so that the last players and singers exit on the final phrases of the chant.

When the chant is over, CAIPHAS, *holding the* C_4 *bell, rings three long tolls.*

After a moment of silence, the play ends.

37. *free*—fair one

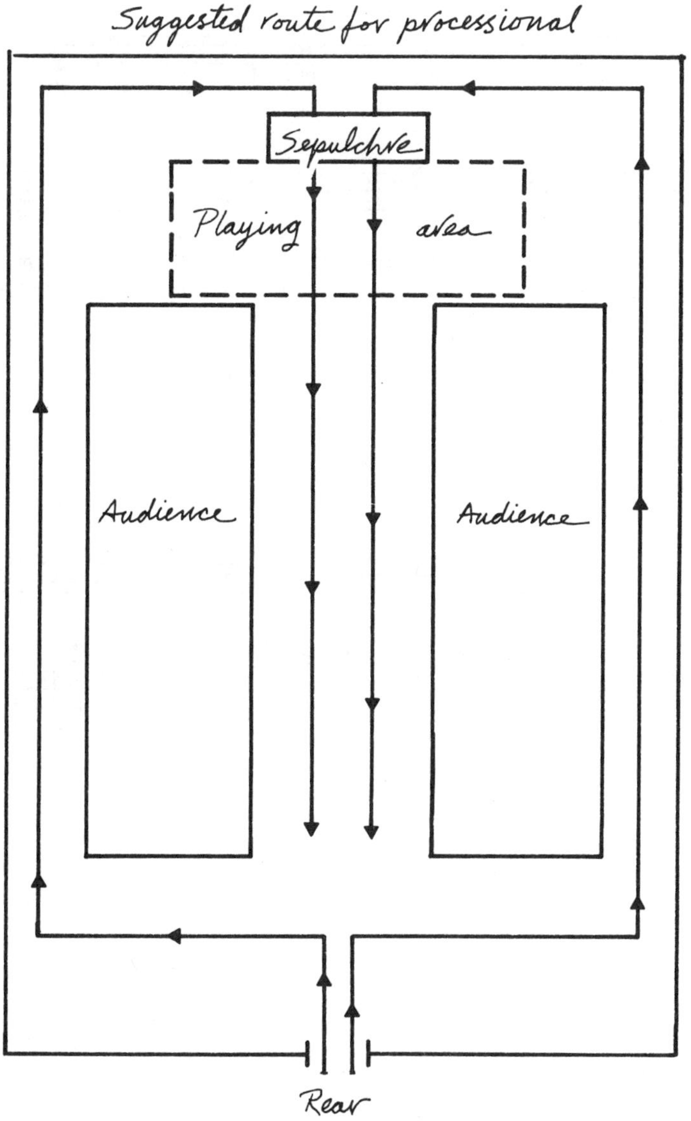
Suggested route for processional
Sepulchre
Playing area
Audience
Audience
Rear

NUMBER 1. REX CAELI, DOMINE

(9th century)

NUMBER 2. L'HOMME ARMÉ

anonymous

NUMBER 3. ALLE PSALLITE CUM LUYA

English 14th century

Al - le - psal - li - te cum lu -
lu - - - - ya, Al - le - lu - - ya,
ya, Al - le con - cre - pan - do psal - li - te cum
Al - le - lu - ya, Al - - - le - lu -
lu - - ya, Al - le -
ya, Al - - le - lu - ya. Al -
cor de - vo - to de - o to - to psal - li - te cum lu - ya.
- le - lu - - - ya, Al -

Al - le psal - li - te cum
Al - - -
- le - lu - - ya, Al - le - lu -
lu - ya,
Al - le -
Al - le psal - li - te cum lu - ya
ya, Al - le - lu - ya, Al -
con - cre - pan - do psal - li - te cum lu - ya,
Al - le con - cre - pan - do
- le - lu - ya, Al - le -
Al - le cor de - vo - to de - o to - to
psal - li - te cum lu - ya,
lu - ya, Al - le - lu -

psal - li - te cum lu - - ya
Al - le cor de - vo - to de - o to - to
- - - ya. Al - - le - lu -
Al - le - lu - - - ya.
psal - li - te cum lu - ya, Al - le - lu - ya.
- - - ya, Al - le - lu - ya.
GONG
DRUM
Roll

NUMBER 4. PARCE, DOMINE

Jacob Obrecht (15th century)

- us es, et mi - se - ri - cors,
- us es, et mi - - se - ri - -
et mi - se - ri -
mi - se - ri - cors, ex -
cors ex - - - au -
cors, ex - au - di
au - - - - - - - - di nos in
- di nos, ex - au - di nos
nos in ae - ter - - num,
ae - ter - - - - - num, Do - mi - ne.
in ae - ter - - num, Do - mi - ne.
Do - - - - mi - - - - ne.

NUMBER 5. TE DEUM

(Gregorian)

WOMEN
Te __ per or - bem ter - ra - rum san - cta __ con - fi - te - tur ec - cle - si - a.
MEN
Pa - - trem __ im - men - sae ma - je - sta - tis.
WOMEN
Ve - ne - ran - dum tu - um ve - rum, et u - ni - cum __ fi - li - um.
MEN
San - - ctum __ quo - que pa - ra - cli - tum __ spi - ri - tum.
WOMEN
Tu __ rex glo - ri - as, __ Chri - ste.
MEN
Tu pa - tris
sem - pi - ter - nus es __ fi - li - us.
WOMEN
Tu ad __
li - be - ran - dum sus - cep - tu - rus ho - - mi - - nem,
non hor - ru - i - sti vir - gi - nis __ u - te - rum.
MEN
Tu de __ vic - to mor - tis a - cu - - le - - o,
a - pe - ru - i - sti cre - den - ti - bus re - gna cae - lo - rum.

WOMEN
Tu ad___ dex - te - ram de - i se - - des___ in glo - ri - a___ pa - tris.
MEN
Iu - dex cre - de - ris es - se ven - tu - rus.
WOMEN
Te er - go quae - su - mus, tu - is fa - mu - lis sub - - - ve - - - ni,
quos pre - ti - o - so san - gui - ne___ re - de - mi - sti.
MEN
Ae - ter - num fac___ cum san - ctis tu - is in glo - ri - a nu - me - ra - ri.
Sal - vum___ fac po - pu - lum tu - um do - mi - ne,___
WOMEN
et be - ne - dic he - re - di - ta - ti - tu - ae.
MEN
Et re - ge e - os,___ et ex - tol - le il - los us - que in ae - ter - num.
WOMEN
Per sin - gu - los di - - - es, be - ne - di - ci - mus te.
MEN
Et lau - da - mus no - men tu - um in sae - cu - lum,

WOMEN
et in sae - cu - lum sae - cu - li. Di - gna - re do - mi - ne di - e
i - - sto sine pec - ca - to nos cu - sto - di - re.
MEN
Mi- se - re re nos - tri do - mi - ne, mi - se - re - re nos - tri.
WOMEN
Fi - at mi - se - ri - cor - di - a tu - a do - mi - ne su - per nos,
quem ad mo - dum spe - ra - vi - mus in te.
ALL
In te do - mi - ne spe - ra - - vi,
non con - fun - dar - in ae - ter - - num.